Poetic Soul

Stevie G.

ISBN: 978-1-4269-3556-5 (sc)
ISBN: 978-1-4269-3557-2 (e-b)

*Our mission is to efficiently provide the world's finest, most comprehensive book publishing
service, enabling every author to experience success. To find out how to publish your book, your
way, and have it available worldwide, visit us online at www.trafford.com*

Trafford rev. 07/16/2010

 www.trafford.com

North America & international
toll-free: 1 888 232 4444 (USA & Canada)
phone: 250 383 6864 ♦ fax: 812 355 4082

Table of Contents

The Wait is Over

Don't look into my eyes and search for a weakness
There is none, so don't seek this
Many years have past and I've lacked in my gift
Paying more attention to a grocery list
I'm a singer, song writer, poetry esquire
And ya damn right my talents for hire
I put it off long enough
Doing chores and stuff
Had two wives and some kids
With skills under my lid
I'm a man with talents that have been waiting inside
To bust out of me and show my creative side
So I'm gonna write and jot write and jot
To fill my pockets with a fat ass knot
No more waiting and procrastinating
And the shit I write will be incubating
That's right pure heat
From pen to pad to audio treats
I bring pain
I bring shame
And I got game
But most of all
I bring shock to your brain
So don't forget me cuz I please to aim
I'm cocked and pointed and Stevie G is the name

Softly Sweet Music

Music is the key, the key to harmony
That special part of me
That lives in the heart of me
Like a beautiful woman you can't ignore
Music, oh sweet music, please do me more
Lay me down and caress my body tonight
Songs of love, the soul's delight
Music, soft music don't conclude
Heartfelt from interlude to prelude
The fingertips of sweet melodies
Massaging my eternal being like raindrops on a flower
As melodic sweetness drifts me away minutes into hours
As the strings soften the moments
As sweet voices sing through components
Music, sweet music you never fail
Sweet music, orgasmic spell
Breaking my body down to nothingness
Sweet music so softly indulging endless
Music infinitely the ultimate sweetness
sweet soft music on a plateau so high
The smile I wear the tears I cry
Sweet music next to me she lies
Sweet music til we close our eyes

Square One

I understand the way you feel
You're a lil caught up
But I keep it real
I can't give you all I have
But you're an intellect
So do the math
One.... she was there before you were
Two.... it wasn't a secret, I told you about her
Three....that doesn't mean you have to go away
Four.... one never knows which way the heart will sway
Five.... good things come to those who wait
And six.... maybe you should rely on fate
An equation has been set
Now are you down
I would do the math
And stick around
But then again, I'm not you
What did you call yourself?
Uhhhh ... three of two
I like you, I think you know that boo
All the talks we have
I know you dig me too
But the table was set from square one
And right now the table setting
Can't be undone
So this is all on you
You can stay or go
But just remember
One never knows
Which way the heart will flow

The View

My eyes behold what Beauty is
Beauty is the sky touching the earth in the horizon
Beauty is the one living flower on a withering branch
My eyes behold what Beauty is
Beauty is the first snow on a winter's night
The first sign of light creeping through the darkest night
Beauty is the adoration you have for the one you love
and the one who loves you back
Beauty is your child at play without a care
And the times you and your child have shared
My eyes behold what Beauty is
Beauty is the face that smiles and melts your heart
Beauty is that precious piece of priceless art
Beauty is the ocean beating against rocky shores
Beauty is an owl's eye staring back at yours
My eyes behold what Beauty is, Beauty is a star lit sky
And snow-capped mountains oh so high
Beauty is a tranquil lake
Beauty is in your mind's eye of the pearly gates
Beauty captivates your soul
Beauty surrounds us, young and old
Beauty is God and
God's Beauty is in you
Beauty is in the eye of the beholder
Because Beauty is God's view

God's Gift From Above

The women in my life are my three girls
Their my heart, my soul, their my world
Three precious gems yet totally different
Three is not a lot but more than sufficient
I pitty the man that doesn't get that chance
To see his daughter go to her first dance
The feeling he has as she walks out the door
Of over protectiveness and a great deal more
But he has watched them grow from little babies
Into the most beautiful and gorgeous lil ladies
You have touched my soul in growing of age
As I've watched you with the turn of each page
God has granted me three wonderful girls
From babies in pigtails to ladies in curls
You are my future and my past
Our love will forever last
Mommies may know, but daddies know best
Where to put things and how to invest
So I invest to you my love
My three beautiful gifts, from God above

Hurt So Bad

When you hurt someone, you only hurt you
Everyone I've ever hurt I felt their pain too
So I ask myself how could I have hurt you
When I didn't even deserve you
You were much better than that hurt
But it didn't matter I still treated you like dirt
Where did I go wrong and why did I go wrong
Hurt is always followed by a sad song
The misery I bestowed upon you
Is the misery I now go through
It's easy to say you're sorry at the time
But for the pain I put you through
The sorrow is now mine
The beautiful woman that I know you are
How could I have left you so scarred
The happiness you once had within
Is now the sadness I live in
The pain, the pressure, and the tears you cried
The treatment you endured, the way I lied
Now is the cloud above me lurking
It's my compensation for all your hurting
I loved you without a clue on how to express
I'm glad now you're free from my stress
Since we've parted our ways
I've had miserable days
After all these years and millions of tears
All the heart wrenching days and nights filled with fear
I feel your pain in my heart and soul
And as I gain age and grow old
I hope you're forgiving me
And let go of the anger you hold
Through all this I've learned to maintain
To respect love, and all love's joy and pain

Nu-Boo

New to me these days
Someone has entered my life
Like beautiful new sun rays
So like the morning light
Glowing like a brand new car
Too sweet, too fine, too sexy, you are
Mmm… I can smell you when you get close to me
Like a field full of jasmine blossoming next to me
Gorgeous, gifted, gracious and black
Caramel, honey-dipped, smooth in fact
You leave that kind of taste in my mouth that makes me go woo!
And I'm just coo-coo for cocoa and craving for you
Give me what I want, make me feel like your man
Me feeling you feeling me is my plan
I put it down like that and make it do what it do
Knock the kinks out the back and make the toes curl too
You're a lady in the streets and a freak in the sheets
And you ride this brotha right til his climax peaks
Now I know why I'm feelin my Nu-Boo
Cuz you got a brotha sayin damn baby, I love you

Stroll

As I sit down to write
About the things in life
They may not be what you wanna hear
But it's my world, my atmosphere
From my life I transpose to a pen
To paper, the thoughts I keep within
It ain't like I gotta bite from yours
Usually when I knock, it opens doors
I've done the wildin out way back then
When I had to get mine
Cuz my pockets was thin
Hangin out under the street lights on Saturday night
Sangin wit da brothas, the harmony was tight
Goin to a party to get in cost twenty-five cents
Walkin to the basement you could smell the incense
Sistas was fly, I mean fly foreal
I'm out there dancin tryin to cop a feel
Shit all hard, I'm all horny
Next thing ya know pussy all up on me
Back then I was pushin a sixty-nine deuce and a quarter
And beatin the brakes off my neighbor's daughter
My grandma, man I miss her, I know she's resting in peace
So sorry that her life had to cease
We used to do some crazy shit to get high
Drink a bottle of cough syrup
And chase it with Bali Hi
Y'all remember the citrus malt liquor
Hoppin Gator, got your ass drunk quicker
But gradually we grow old and change
And before you know it our lives rearranged
Some go east, some go west
Some kiss ass just to impress
This one north and that one south
Didn't make no difference long as we got out

We either learned our lessons or went straight to jail
Or died and went straight to hell
But god knows growin up was fun
Some shit ya did wise, some shit ya did dumb
My mom always schooled me on what life could do
It could give you opportunity and break ya down too
So I'm glad I could take ya down the memory lane stroll
So you could read my life and the stages unfold
I'm done, I'm gonna lay the pen down
But it ain't over, I'm just done for now

The Heat

The hotter the wetter, the tighter the better
C'mon cutie, let's lock up together
I wanna make you feel love, this is a real love
We fit like a body glove
It's a redbone connection
You're on top and moving in the right direction
It was an omen for you and I to meet
That's why the Isley Brothers wrote Between the Sheets
Don't reach over and grab your gear, dear
I ain't through, I got more work to do here
Let me give you a lesson in lovin
It starts with a kiss then some huggin and rubbin
Then the buttons pop, the legs unlock
And my anatomy gets hard like a rock
After tonight I'll be the one you miss
But like Mary J said, Reminisce, Reminisce, Reminisce

Crying Heart

Misty eyed yet I smile inside
In love but it's a rollercoaster ride
To love her is my destiny
I'm in this love but where is she
Alone in love is where I'm at
To visualize her love
I have to go way back
I haven't felt her love in a while
Hurt but I maintain my smile
Impatient maybe , but I don't think so
We've had more than enough time for love to grow
But it's not growing it's in reverse
Just think if I had it
You'd have the universe
But this is how I love you so
 I love you enough not to let you go
You might call it weak and afraid to lose
I call it holding on and that's what I do
But a fool can only go so far
And so far is approximately where we are
I think we've had enough, don't you?
Of pretending that you love me too
So I'm going to let you go, I know it will hurt so
I can't make you love me and this we both know
So this is my goodbye to the love inside
And as I write these words I can feel my heart cry
It's the end for me I'm done, no more
And to this love I close the door
This chapter of my life is through
And all I wish is the best for you

PS: I never knew from the start
That you would bring tears to my heart

Just Like You

I'm a big man, the rock you lean on
The strong arm you depend on
The shoulder you cry on
And who's love you rely on
I'm your protector when in need
The man who planted our seed
The father yes indeed
But I am human just like you
I have feelings as you do
I may be your rock
But rocks crumble too
Look at my tear-stained cheek
Lets you know my shield can leak
I stand here solid as an oak
Never ever with loss of hope
But I hurt like you do
My heart aches too
I hold you when you cry
I'm your front when you're shy
When you shed tears I hold you tight
But who holds me when I cry at night
Hiding not wanting you to know
That your man has pains and sorrows
There's a sensitive man in me
Hidden by my masculinity
I have feelings just like you
Just like you my heart breaks too
So does this mean that you're my oak
Or does it mean you're my hope
Did you ever think I may need to lean on you
You have no idea the impact you have
And how I rely on you just being you
Trying to hide signs when I seem weak
Making sure with you I'm complete

So let me turn to you
For you are my need too
I'm just like you, feeling just like you do

There She Goes Again

There she goes again
Bringing up that same ole shit and then
Wanting me to caress her body that night
After that long drawn out fight
There she goes again
Creeping up on me in bed
Her leg wrapping around my legs
Expecting me to forget the earlier shit
But the leg feels good so, I hit it
There she goes again
Getting on top of me and looking in my eyes
And saying, daddy you like the way I ride
When I climaxed so did she
Then she looks at me and says, I gotta pee
There she goes again
Screaming cuz I left the seat up
Cuz her ass got all wet up
So I laugh when I hear the splash
While she's screaming like she has whiplash
There she goes again
Mad at me once more
Screaming and slamming doors
Angry and won't speak to me
So I put my arms around her gently
But she shrugs me off a tad
I don't really think she's mad
There she goes again
Asking me to put my arms back
But instead I kiss the small of her back
And she turns and looks at me
And says, I love you baby
There she goes again
Cold as ice then hot as fire
There she goes again

Being my heart's desire
Here I go again
Loving her cuz
There she goes again

Aimless

What is your purpose in your time here
Not in this moment but in your existence
Have you exercised your all
Have you been more than a little persistent
Have you dug and pushed scratched and clawed
And yet you maintain and entertain you're flaws
Has life not slapped you in the face with learned lessons
Has God not rained upon you his blessings
When will you learn to cut the negative matter
When will your mind begin to collect and gather
The positive side of a day
And turn a cheek to the negative way
You have so much to offer you're existence here
Why give so much up to your fears
You are just living life in God's abyss
Why not give it you're all
Not to is aimless

Self Toast

I bend over backward to do what's right
And at all times I maintain and keep my game tight
When I say game I don't mean gaming you
It means just doin me, that's what I do
If I don't do me , who else will ?
Keep myself groomed especially my skills
I'd rather work and write than fuss and fight
But if need be your gonna get argument, right?
I can be you're lovable huggable teddy bear
But if rubbed the wrong way, you're worst nightmare
I won't get off into the negative
Too much shit pushes me to sedatives
And I don't do drugs I like it natural
And when I write I keep it factual
I'm not writing about shit right now, but me
But once in a while Stevie G gotta love Stevie G
I know I get mad love from all my peeps too
But if I didn't love me, would you?
I'm keepin it real not trying to fabricate a story
Actually bullshit and fake shit bore me
So this poem is to self roast the host with the most
And raise my glass high to toast
The C.E.O the man yall know
Stevie G the most original

When Love Comes

When love comes
You'll know it has
Love is a strength you can't let pass
When love comes
It will control your mindset
Love is the hearts finger print
When love comes
It's the basis of motivation
The expression of every notation
When love comes
Your desires expand
That mushy feeling between and woman and man
When love comes
Beware of the haters
The home breakers, the instigators
When love comes
Forget the haters
For love changes your behavior
When love comes
It touches the soul
It makes understanding a mutual goal
When love comes
It gets two in sync
It changes the way you think
When love comes
It's a new way to live
A new reason to give
When love comes
It's the new you
Then the words, I do
When love comes
It's one of life's greatest lessons
It's the greatest of God's blessings
When love comes

When Rain Falls

When rain falls and I'm all alone
With no you to hold
It's too quiet in my home
I hear the rain beating against my window pane
But you're not here so it's driving me insane
When the rain falls
And love calls
 Existing in solitude
Has exhausted my joyful mood
 When rain falls
Then you call
It makes me crave you more
And rainfall without you has become a bore
Don't get me wrong
I love the rain fall
I just love having you here
When it falls, that's all

She's Amazing Isn't She

How she laughs trying to hide her anger
When you do one of the stupid things you do
How when you call her she won't answer
But has to hold her hand back with the other hand
Just not to pick up your phone call
I just don't understand what makes her tick
But never the less
She's amazing isn't she
When she calls you and you don't answer her call
And no matter what you were doing at the time
It had to involve some wrong doing on your part
When actually you were on the phone ordering
A dozen long stem roses just for her being her
But in her eyes it's just another one of your lies
Until of course she receives the roses
Then you're the sweetest and
She's amazing isn't she
She loves you and you know she does
And you love her and she knows you do
But yet you two play the tit for tat game
You don't contact her and she doesn't contact you
And as usual you have to break the ice and call because she
won't
And she is sitting by the phone in stubborn mode
Knowing she wants to hear your voice but stuck in denial
Crazy isn't she but this woman, lawd this woman
She's amazing isn't she
I love this woman no matter how the tables turn
Even in all I expect her to do and knows she will
I still come back for more and more of her craziness
It's said you have to take the bitter with the sweet
But her bitter is sweet to taste
And love has shown me that no matter how love confronts
you

Let love do exactly what it does and that's simply love
So when your woman acts like she's a lil buggy
It's not buggy it's just that
She's amazing isn't she

Blessings

I was driving my car this morning
And I noticed how beautiful the trees looked in bloom
And realized I was blessed enough to see a new sunlight
And possibly the rising of a new moon
When getting up this morning and putting my feet on the floor
I understood my blessings from God once more
I called my daughter this morning and she is doing fine
God has blessed my children time after time after time
As I creep through life's middle ages
God has blessed me throughout the stages
As I arrived at my job today ready to face the stress
I embraced my thoughts and I know just to have a job I'm blessed
The residue of God's work on earth are a wonder for the eye to view
But the blessings from above are only cherished by few
Imagine life not being blessed at all
Think of how far you would fall
The saying goes "count your blessings"
In counting, my biggest blessing is learning from life's lessons
I'm blessed to have a relationship with God in my life
My next blessing I hope, is a loving wife

Sista-Hood

Ummmm !!! girl dat ass framed in chocolate thighs
Got brotha's breakin necks
And sista's envious eyed
Walk mami, walk for me boo
Got brotha's wreckin cars tryin to get at you
Sexy from yo head to yo manicured toes, wrapped in stiletto's,
Eatin ho ho's, and gorgeous in da ghetto
You can take a sista out da ghetto
But, da ghetto grows on in a sista
Me, I'd rather have a sista from round da way
She gonna have my back all damn day
She's works it! street and corporate too
Off work, smokin a black and drankin a brew
She got a lil 3 series beamer wit a drop top
She always got game so I call her, can't stop, won't stop!
She da kinda sista that get a brotha open
Got most of em hopin and all of em scopin
Dis sista is fine as frog hair
Da essence of ghetto air
She is sista-hood

The Pathway

Romance, love has enhanced
Life is a gamble left to chance
Promises kept and promises failed
Due to excuses lacking details
I love you... wow!!!
These three words
So strong the meaning
But over used and over heard
I recognize love at it's best
Shouldn't I ?
I've been there more than once in my lifetime
We all endure the happiness and pain
That love's agony and ecstasy have drained
Peeling back the layers of life's avenues
Recalling personalities, characteristics, and attitudes
Exposing life's highs and lows
But no need for worry, that's just the way life goes
Hold on to what you have
You may never get another chance
Like I said at the start
Love can be enhanced
Wake up !!
Life is filled with surprises
Elements of life wear many disguises
But don't let that stop you from taking risks
Because, your fate and dreams just might be missed

How I See You

First I had to intake your smile
It let me know your heart is larger than a mile
Then I gazed into your eyes
And there I found the soul's prize
And as you talked I was mesmerized by your lips
And it gets better as I move south to the hips
Anyway, back to the lips... and why they captured me
Your voice was sweet and sounded oh so softly
As our conversation started to climb
I realized this woman has a wonderful mind
I was deeply impressed by your looks and wisdom
I think you're the perfect fit for my kingdom
You're almost mapped out, I'm half way finished
I noticed you have beautiful skin barely a blemish
You're all good from the neck up
You deserves to where the crown
Now that the north is done
Let's see how the south gets down
Your neckline is one of sensuality
Approaching your voluptuous breast
Where I long to lay my head to listen to your heart confess
From your breast to your hips I'll massage so tenderly
And kiss every inch in between until you submit to me
Kissing you is my pleasure especially in your favorite place
And how much joy I get seeing pleasure on your face
Then rub you down with hot oil until your toes my fingers
meet
And suck each and every toe on those very pretty feet
Now that I've described you exactly to a tee
Perfection is your description most definitely
My expression are real and always sincere and true
Explains the way I feel on how I see you

Its Growing

Affection is the complexion of these writings by me
Because everyday my heart warms more for she
I laugh endlessly for countless days and nights
Effortlessly she spreads joy into my life
Without even knowing what she does to this brother
She's sets the stage and finally we're growing to lovers
Oooooh wee!! their growing my desires and needs
She's giving me visions of white beaches and exotic palm trees
Yes, some one on one time just you and I
Not over the phone but under some starlit skies
I'm feeling romantic I wanna make love to your mind
Then tear your body down when you send the right signs
I feel something growing from thin to wide
Do you know what my heart is holding on the inside?
The growth of love
It's growing

It Occurred To Me

This morning while thinking
Love is here now, but could be gone in an inkling
That God will bless me with a woman so sweet
Just gorgeous, every man's eye treat
A woman that can teach me more on how to be a man
To be patient, to trust, and to understand
It occurred to me
As I scrolled back through the decades
How life could be such a stifling maze
How learning from lessons has paid off
How a woman's touch can be so soft
How dreams can be lost and cause regret
How amazing the mind is to not let us forget
It occurred to me
My children God's greatest gift to me
That I adore completely
That have started new family in replica of me
They will endure more and see more than I had to see
Precious they are in this cold, cold world
Two strong boys and two beautiful girls
As they grow older they know not what they face
This world is not sugary and not lace
It occurred to me
That my God has a place for me
A place I won't regret to be
He'll place a woman in my life to share
His blessings, my heart, and his breath of air
He's watching as I write these lines
He's been watching all the time
Guiding me through the storms of life
When blinded he has been my sight
It occurred to me
God has always been beside me
Loving me and guiding me

I'm Only a Man

I'm only being exactly who I am
Never perfect just a man
Wanting what's right to those I hold dear
Doing all I can to understand our atmosphere
But at the same time, I'm only a man
Things get difficult for a man as well
We suffer life's issues and we go through our own hell
We love deep, don't sleep
We need love and yes, we creep
But women do the same shit
Their just much the better advocate
We do our thing thoughtless in our approach
What we need in our lives is a female creep coach
And yes, I'm still a man
Men don't really want to see their women hurt
It depends on how much will power we have
Or how short the mini skirt
Men have been known to stray
But some ladies give us reasons to stay away
I'm not making an excuse
For situations I've been known to abuse
Yet, I'm only a man
We still want you happy and as always we got your back
And when we show our love we actually want love back
You see , we too have sensitive sides
But women only see what they want through their eyes
We can't help the picture they paint
We never claimed to be saints
Never ! I'm only a man
Men are from Mars and women from Venus
But we already knew that
 Women have a vagina and men a penis
We need no books to show and prove this fact
Shit!! just keep a sharp eye on how we act

I'm a man and I fucked up some
But when it all boils down you are the one and only one
And yes, I'm only a man

Natural Bling-Bling

I know a sister, she's an exceptional lady
Skin as smooth as grandma's gravy
She's got that huge heart that thumps really loud
The kind of lady that stands out in a mass crowd
I would love to be her man but that's not a reality
She has a husband so I can't even be, her man to be
I know I could but maybe she thinks not
But then she didn't know me when she tied the knot
She's an intellect and witty shining like brand new
Diamonds in her ears…oh, in her lip too
Did I not mention fine .. well this woman is hot
Makes you have to double take your woman
To see what you've got
Sometime we let the special ones pass us right by
But not this time you're like hanging on my eye
I have to give it to you you've got my attention
But I got eyes on me too or did I forget to mention
So don't sleep baby boo because I'm watching you
So make sure hubby makes it do what it do
So I'm going to close in saying one more thing
You don't need diamonds, you got that natural bling-bling

The Hidden Flower

I see you over there hiding behind the other flowers
I've watched you grow with each rain shower
Hiding by day expressing by night
Running from the sun and soaking in the moonlight
Everyone adores you look at our smiles
Growing all around you like weeds in the wild
Ooooh honey child what flower are you
Got bees all around you doin what they do
The smell the sweet aroma you exhaust like mist
Do you understand why we act like this
Well, you need not hide your loveliness any longer
Beautiful hidden, I wonder
Why the hidden feelings are for you
When you express love more than the other flowers do
You really do stand out in the bunch
Perhaps this is why you're loved so much
Beautiful in color vibrant in growth
You have been watched much more than most
Now you stand in the forefront and the others behind
All that know you knew this was a matter of time.
So, live hidden flower, love hidden flower, and hide no more
Stand proud with petals smiling for you are adored

Blessed With a Sister

The greatest gift from god to man is you
The flower of the earth sparkled with morning dew
Soft to touch so delicate you are
Nothing as bright to me, not even a shining star
Easy to view admired by all
Colorful and brisk like foliage in fall
Warm and sensual as that of a spring night
Graceful as an eagle gliding in flight
Beautiful cocoa caramel and creamy
Like a summer's eve, hot and steamy
The love of some the envy of most
Next to my heart I hold you close
Black woman you are
The brightest of all stars
Proud and erect with your stance so tall
The most gorgeous woman of them all
A daughter a mother a sister a niece
A god send a symbol of peace
A queen next to me on my throne
The woman I need to help build my home
Black woman you are the essence of earth
And underestimated is your worth
I love you black woman you are to me
My life my love my family

Turned the Love Off

When that feeling hits you and your stomach turns
And you lose that love , the love you yearn
The tears form but they don't fall
And you lie in bed curled in a ball
All your thoughts are really bad
Even your good thoughts keep you sad
It's going to be hard but you gear up for pain
The more you try and convince you
The more insane
Doing your best to forget the love you have
But it's harder than Chinese arithmetic
Yeah it's just that bad
Well it's over now no sense in tears
It's useless lying here counting your fears
It was a love a love so soft
But someone has turned the love off

Simply Love

Two hearts beating together as one
Intertwined and synchronized, the tandem
Two bodies tingling in harmonic ecstasy
Each heart and soul investigating
Every inch they lay woven and meshed
At peace without complex
The music is perfect the lighting just right
As they lay til dark night meets daylight
A night of love has creped into the next day
Their mood has not changed so yet they lay
Love has taken over their mindset
Continuously they embrace without regret
Sensual moans and groans and the words I love you
 The sweetest composition coming from the bedroom
 Abundant admiration in loves atmosphere
Keeps the minds clear and the hearts near
As they doze off to sleep still entangled
With one another
They dream of an encore as true lovers
And another perfect day into night
As flawless as two doves in flight
For them dreams have become reality
They have conquered and now own loves mentality
Love the greatest gift to mankind
God's love is great at all times

The Cake Is So Sweet

Is it true we want our cake to eat it too ?
I would eat it, wouldn't you ?
Maybe I'm a lil selfish for my own good
But never am I left standing saying
Should, could or would
Yes I wear my hat to the side
And I may even glide when I stride
But that's why I got the extra cake
I keep it real, I don't do fake
I don't do fake doesn't mean I don't lie
I've been known to have a few
Inaccurate alibi's
So please know that I am not of the angelic
But I know a few, of me they relic
Can't hold back what you feel sometime
Ya gotta go for it so I go for mine
After you read this don't get your panties in a bunch
It's just the way the cake crumbs crumble
And the cookies crunch
We all are guilty of doing some shit
I guess I'm guilty of writing this poem
But we'll all get over it
It's only some small stuff it will go away
But I'm going to be the same the next day the next day
And the next day.
Cause the cake is so damn sweet

I Miss You

I don't understand where I went so wrong
To damage a love I thought was so strong
You owned my heart and you know that
Now my heart is lonely and again in black
It felt good last night to laugh with you again
But I woke up this morning still wondering
It's really tough loving someone
And not knowing where you stand
Hoping and praying she still remembers our plans
You see, it's not talking to you I miss
It's you being who you were, I miss
I just have this to say and I'm done
Am I or am I not still the one?
I miss you!

Loaf of Love

Love is such a powerful attribute
Gifted by our Heavenly Father
Love shared, a sacred institute
Everything primed in our hearts
Is thought out in our minds
And dissected part by part
And exercised in everyday living
Which is taken in by the love we're given
You look in her eyes and she in yours
Then love takes over and you crave more and more
I asked God to show me all about love
 He blessed me with the ingredients of what love is made of
A cup of compassion and two cups of trust
Half a cup of patience and a dash of peace a must
A listening ear and an open heart an addition so pure
Omit the jealousy and envy to help the love endure
God's contents of love and the preparation
Are gifted to you through spiritual dedication
Once you've sifted stirred and mixed
 Tossed and folded and twists
And then you add God into your daily lives
It will slowly start to rise
And when it's finished and all complete
It's true love, our destiny
Gods gifts to us are peaceful and pure
No matter who we are, rich or poor
Love is a gift we should always treasure
It's graceful harmonious and always our pleasure

My Heart Desires

Who says I have to love you because you love me
When all I have to do is live, die, be black, and be me
Why do I have to cry when you feel pain
And when you cry should I feel shame
Should I feel what you feel when you feel what you do
Or should I listen to my heart when it tells me who
To care for to be near to share with I swear
I can't help it when what I do brings your eyes to tears
So if you're angry with me I don't understand why
I have to follow my heart I can't live a lie
And tell you something we know isn't true
Three simple words I love you
I can't tell you what it is I don't feel
If you're not what I want and you don't appeal
To what my hearts desires and what my soul adores
Can I help it that I'm craving much, much more
It really is useless for you to cry the blues
Because my heart has already chosen who it wanted to
choose
I'm not saying these things to be mean or cruel
And I definitely don't want you to think that you have been a
fool
I think you're beautiful and lovely but just not for me
But I'm sure you'll find someone to love you
And love you properly

The Journey

On the way over I stopped and seen
Somebody on the other side
Where the grass was green
Isn't it funny what life can throw your way
One day happy the next in disarray
It's hard keeping someone happy
When you're not happy with self
Sometime you gotta do what you gotta do
Based on the cards you're dealt
Let's sit down and check life and life's philosophy
And you and I can mull over what life is supposed to be
I say life is simple and take it with a grain of salt
And you think life is all you can cram up in bank vault
Money can't buy you your next breath
If god wants to take it away
But you can purchase your next breath
If you fall to your knees and pray
I've done something's I'm not proud of
And things that weren't so cool
I've even done something's
That some might render cruel
But life goes and continues to move along
Just as long as lessons are learned
And life doesn't sing the same old songs
So be the go getter somewhat the heavy hitter
And not the alternative the infamous bull shitter
 Live life to the fullest and take the bull by the horns
Life is a bed of roses but roses do have thorns
And as you travel through your life
Remember you've been warned
And the journey doesn't end
Until God says when....

Love Lotto

Picture waking up one morning debt free
Due to your winning ticket in the lottery
Twenty million and problems down the drain
All that glitters is gold
And now you're not so plain
What ya gonna do with twenty mill cold cash
I know what I'm gonna do
Take care of my wife's fine ass
It's cause for celebration
Time for a Mr. and Mrs. collaboration
Get together and discuss our future plans
Cause this damn money is burning a hole in my hand
She wants a brand new home with elegant style
A brand new Mercedes would make this brotha smile
But these are material things in life
I want real quality time with my wife
And I'm gonna get that, I don't work no more
We're going to buy an island with sensual shores
And take long, long walks on our beaches
And everything we need to know about us
We'll teach us
Shit, I didn't realize the meaning of living with you
See what a lil quality time can do
We didn't need money to share this time
But all the everyday shit can keep one blind
Blind enough to make you disregard her worth
You never needed money to make it work
She just wants love that's all she ever ask for
And now she can get that and a whole lot more
A lil more finance will make it all the more sweet
But right now I don't have to work
So imma go back to sleep

Days Gone By

Days gone by
I hold a precious gift
In my soul so high
This gift called expression
Alleviates all my depression
Through my heart and deep in my soul
My inner strength plays It's role
Through my heart then my mind
Their processed to pen then paper
Through your eyes to the mist of your mind
Days gone by

Smile Please

Smile please things could be worse
Take your life for what it's worth
You may think things are going bad for you
If you only knew what others go through
Grab hold of yourself embrace your being
Don't run from your problems
It's useless fleeing
Smile please today is your day
Life is good and things are going your way
Help somebody, do something good and kind
And in them a friend you may find
It doesn't hurt at all to be nice
What do you benefit being cold as ice
Smile please life is not that hard
Sometime it's ok to let down your guard
There is a homeless family with no food to eat
Tired and hungry walking the streets
Not knowing when they can feed their child
And you have a nerve not to wear a smile
Smile please, it's easier to
A little less complaining when something happens to you
Do you not have a pot to piss in nor a window to throw it out
If not I guess you have good reason to pout
What if you had no pot and no window
Not even a house or a home to go into
Then we could see a reason for no smile
For some this is a way of life not a life style
Smile please God loves us all
Even though hard times, smile on and stand tall
Be patient and love your neighbor
And follow the wishes of our savior
Those days when there seems to be nothing but stressing
Just remember in the storm there's always a blessing
So open your heart and smile for a while
Smile please smile

Body Language

Lay down baby and relax
Daddy wants to do something to ya
To make your body relapse
Hold on tight boo ride me right
I'm all yours take me on loves flight
Let me drop to my knees
And kiss you with these
Hot wet succulent lips
On that fever between your hips
This is your night baby girl
And I aim to rock your world
Beautiful gorgeous chocolate tan
You want this sexy butter pecan man
I'm kissing you north to south east to west
Round your back then back to your breast
Long slow powerful strokes and thrust
All the way till your climax busts
Take all your pain away
And leave you in complete ecstasy
Treat your body so correct
Give you that toe curling effect
Put you into total satisfaction
Multiple orgasmic reactions
Then let you get your rest
Laying your head on my chest
And wait for you to awake
Then we'll do a second take
Just to please you is my quest
And doing this all over again is the rest

Unforgiving

What have I done to you baby
Have I broken your heart
I read the locket you made me
It's stays close to my heart
Oh my God, I never meant to burden you
Let me get in a word or two
About how I truly feel
Expression signed and sealed
You are special to me for life
I've paid a special price
By opening my heart wide
By turning off my pride
Baby you are my essentials
My future my mementos
My nights and my days
The one that never goes astray
You lead me in paths I never thought I'd travel
Sometime the road is smooth some as rough as gravel
But through all the thick and thin
I have your special peace within
The God given love I have for you
Have gotten me through a rough time or two
So please forgive me if I've taken you to a rocky place
As I wipe the tear stains from your lovely face
She wasn't worth the tears you shed
I never listened to a word you said
 The words you said when we were new
And how you knew our love was true
It was never meant to be like this
To break your heart and steal your gift
The gift that you and I have shared
It's almost as if I never cared
But I do love you and I hope you see that
Through this poem I write to you in black

This was never ever worth the risk
Of losing your love and feeling like this
Just so you know I'll love you for life
Please forgive me my darling wife...

Dimples on My Mind

In light of all the things in life
The most difficult thing
Was in my forty's, leaving my wife
And it was not because I loved her so much
It was being so used to her
 The traditional day to day and such
At first I surrounded myself in solitude
And that had me in the most miserable mood
Then as the months past by
The misery increased along with my
Tear drenched eyes
 Many tears rolled down across my cheeks
From day to day and week to week
So tired of being tired of me
I needed a drastic change and quickly
So I picked myself up and shook myself out
Got rid of the pity and lost the doubt
I said to myself you're a man you're single
So off to the club I went to mingle
And once I got there ooooh I swear
The women were all up in there
So I shrugged my shoulders to wake up my mack
And once I did digits racked in stacks
So I talked to these women and they boosted my moral
But I couldn't hurt these sisters I'm not that foul
So I picked and chose and chose and picked
Some skinny some chocolate
Some caramel some thick
But I'm a man that's satisfied with one
And this is where the hunt begun
For a woman so sweet so soft and so true
And doesn't mind a hundred times saying I love you
One with a big heart and a stable life
That I wouldn't mind calling my wife

So I took them in,the notes and phone calls
But this beat the old me of climbing the walls
So one day I must admit while surfing the internet
I saw a photo that made me sweat
And this picture I couldn't forget
She was gorgeous from bottom to top
And my thoughts of her just wouldn't stop
So I sent her my number via yahoo.com
But she wouldn't give me a minute of her time
But I kept up the pursuit I'm just that kind of dude
I didn't get pushy and I never got rude
And then one day I made her smile
And after that oooh oooh child
Things were going to get easier
I made her know by verbally pleasing her
I broke her mind down first
And the old bubble burst
Our conversations grew and grew day by day
And I started thinking of her in a different way
She was definitely wifey material
We even liked the same cereal
Wow.. I was really falling for this chick
This here shit was really getting thick
She and I were enjoying our phone time so
There was a lot to cover and a lot to get to know
So we did that and this is where we are now
In love with each other and all I can say is wow
And every time I look at her picture I say
Dimples on my mind today...

Ear Drops

There I go ..there I go ..there I go do the words ring a bell
They are to "Moody's Mood for Love", and I know them very well
My mom played it all my life, along with Dakota Staton's "Give Me the Simple Life"
Listen to the content in the lyrics not only should your ears but your heart should hear it
Ya just can't bob your head and vibe to a beat
The lyrics of the song are the real heart beat
Think about the songs back in the day
I know I can't forget and they went this way
Don't you know I heard it through the grapevine
And between love and hate there's a thin line
If you don't know me by now
Oh yeah, and betcha by golly wow
Sparkle in your eyes and my ..my.. my.. my ..my.. my ..my
Is this taking ya back
How about the Temps sangin Psychadelic Shack
Soften it up a touch with let's just kiss and say goodbye
And take it way the hell back with smoke gets in your eye
These songs are embedded in the archives of my memories
Turn back the hands time and Sam Cooke's you send me
Earth, Wind, and Fire said, Keep your head to the sky
And then they gave you the reason why
And let's not leave out brotha Luther Vandross
He didn't sing this but we were closer than close
But he did sing if only for one night
And how da hell could we forget skin tight
This is my lil blast from da past
Just a lil history for dat ass
I'll come back another day
But for today, I did it my way…

The Sensational You

You are my tranquil moments
In time when I need to ease my pain
Granted to me by God you've come
A precious flower withered none
Only you know my weakness
My heart my fears I speak this
To the sensational you
You the sensational
Captivating me so thorough
Entering my heart like there is no tomorrow
Pleasuring me without a single touch
The treasure of my thoughts
In you lies my faith and trust
This is loves power over lust
Open your hands to hold my heart
I pray our love will never part

The Dream Heaven vs. Hell

It's black in the abyss
Like that of a quiet storm
My eyes are not closed
Their getting close, I'm being drawn
I try to move away but my legs won't go
I need to shield myself
Now the bright lights glow
Heaven is above me
Hell is below
I'm utterly confused
No idea which way I should go
God is pulling me north
Satan pulling south
I think I want the right path
But my mind feels inside out
The choices are good versus bad
Happiness versus sad
Life's ultimatums can sometime be a drag
I think I'll hold my head up
And live my life correct
I can't seem to comprehend
Satan's dialect
I want to be a good man
And live my life right
With Satan on my left and God on my right
How does one live correct
Being pulled from right to left
My heart belongs to God
But Satan has my mind in check
One day I'll out grow this fear
And choose one way to live
I think I'll hold my God so dear
And Satan I'll forgive

With Love Woman

Whewwww ! woman if you only knew
When you walk across a room
What you put my body through
Damn I'm having trouble thinking of what to say
can't concentrate
My minds in disarray
Wanting to say I love you
Don't want your head to swell
You know I hate to say this
But you got me weak as hell
Short fat thin or tall
Means nothing to me
I don't think that small
Lies alibis cutie pies with no ties
I'm ready to commit
don't matter about your size
I need real love
Ummmmm so sweet
I can't handle another twenty year repeat
I want to see my woman glow
I want to see how much we grow
Not worried about when she gets old
Not concerned with her lil jelly roll
I love her so no matter what
And she loves me even with my beer gut
This is called unconditional
Our love, fact not fictional
Embrace love as though it's the last breath
I love you baby and I'm truly blessed
With love woman

Togetherness

Togetherness is shared by two people to facilitate loneliness
Loneliness is apprehended and altered by togetherness
We share our heart with ones we love and desire
Which togetherness has brought us to appreciate and admire
Our hearts intertwine in a tandem melody
While beating in a perfect flowing harmony
God has blessed us with the companionship of one another
And togetherness has issued us a license as true lovers
Over time we have become one body of two
Now loneliness is meaningless and selfishness is taboo
For us togetherness is our life line , it's our blood
Without it we'd be like, where is the love
We hold on tight and interlock our sacred hearts
For in togetherness there is no far apart

One Love

What if love was all you had left
What would you do?
No money no homes no cars
Just her and you
No where to cheat
No lots of fish in the sea
Just one man one woman
One L-O-V-E
You have to have conversation
Your left with no choices
Just two people only two voices
No others to hug no mom dad or child
Just us two and only two smiles
Happy sad sickness and health
Just the two of us and love is our wealth
No jobs no rat race
No dog eat dog world
Just you yourself herself your girl
No time to waste time is not of the essence
Just you your girl your world
And God's blessings
Just you two together in your dwelling
No bugaboo's and pest and sales people selling
Clothes cars food or service
Just a pure calm nothing to make you nervous
God's gift to you is she
And she you
No worries problems nor tears
Just you for her and her for you
How precious the gift of God can be
Where there used to be two now there is three...

Dear Me

Dear me, I'm writing this letter to myself
In search of my worth and my wealth
I'm feeling good about me, aren't you?
But others don't really have a clue
Who am I, I'm asking of me
Am I a vision of what the eye may see?
Or an illusion a mass of air
Olive toned black is my hair
I'm filled with thoughts that rush my mind
And in these thoughts treasures I find
Will I be selfish or will I share
The treasures of my thoughts I'll bear
I live my life mostly in loneliness
It's not a curse by God I'm blessed
I need to peek inside my brain
Where my memories have staked their claim
A loss for words every now and then
Will let most know the mood I'm in
I seek for refuge that lies within
A place I might begin my end
In search to find a cure for the fear of death
Causes me to cherish every breath
The kiss of life is the love I've shared
Nothing greater can compare
It may not glitter like gold should
Unfortunately all we do in life is not good
But I hang the small things in a good place
Nothing more precious than a smile on a face
As I approach the peak of life's conclusion
And look back on much of my confusion
This road of life, this roller coaster ride
God has been with me step by step, stride for stride
So I write this letter to myself
To remind me God has given me health

And as I bring me to a close
Looking down the avenues I've chose
Lets me know I wasn't by myself
Which brings me back to my health
This is my God given wealth
Dear me, I'm writing this letter to myself

Lust versus Love versus In Love

Love can creep up in multiple forms
It never comes in exact tandems
And always out of the norm
It's attributes are meant to confuse
Lust versus love versus in love
Heartbreak lies in what you choose
Carefully observe the outer being
Beauty is only skin deep
Your heart and soul pleading
The exterior is so appealing
The walk the talk
You contemplate the feeling
While the interior is being underestimated
The exterior is being overly investigated
Though precious to the eye
Those motivating thighs
The beautiful smile
Is this where lust hides
Or where love lies
Confusing isn't it?
Lust versus love versus in love
Love lives in the heart and lust in the brain
All though alike love and lust are never the same

About the Author

Steven White was born in Plainfield, New Jersey, and attended Plainfield Public Schools. His passion for music and song writing inspired him to incorporate those styles of writing into his poetry. He is supported by his children, grandchildren, siblings, and a host of close friends.